Social Media for the Soul Vol. 1

Compiled by Renee Henderson

Guardian House

Social Media for the Soul Vol. 1
Compiled by Renee Henderson

ISBN: 978-0-9941119-9-9
Henderson, Renee, 1969-
Social Media for the Soul Vol. 1/ Renee Henderson.
North Island, New Zealand
Originally Published: 2016.

Published in 2016 by Guardian House
www.guardianhouse.tumblr.com
AUCKLAND, NEW ZEALAND

CAUTION: The information given in this book is not intended to act as a
substitute for medical treatment, nor can it be used for diagnosis

Social Media for the Soul Vol. 1

Compiled by Renee Henderson

Guardian House

About the Author

The Castles we live in today, were first built in the air... live your dreams.

— Renee Henderson

Renee Henderson is a writer, author, consultant, teacher, profiler and healer. She is also a Photographer, Contemporary Abstract Artist, Digital Artist. Renee is an international writer and author of book titles such as:

- Who Stole My Energy?

- You Can Transform Your Life

- What is a Medium?
  Uncensored Psychic Medium

- Wisdom
  - Wisdom of Nature
  - Wisdom of Children

- The Healing Art
  Contemporary Art, Photography, Digital Art. This is a story, told in words, photography, digital art and contemporary art, of Renee's journey through the darkness of severe depression and Borderline Personality Disorder, and the roller-coaster ride that she experienced and continues to live with daily. Mental Health does not have to be a dirty word, if so many continue to think this old school way of thought then there is no room to heal the soul and self and then there is no room to hope for a better tomorrow. (The Healing Art is in Full Colour). *This book is presently out of print please see; Guardian House Website www.guardianhouse.tumblr.com to find out where you can purchase the pieces of Art from the book 'The Healing Art' and more.*

- Social Media for the Soul Vol. 1

- Social Media for the Soul Vol. 2

Even through the following obstacles Renee continues to write, teach, profile and more. If you wish to do something you find a way, if you don't wish to do something you will always find excuses.

Renee writes to motivate and inspire others, as Renee lives with Fibromyalgia and severe pain daily. Fibromyalgia can be an extremely painful and exhausting condition, and for some it can cause disability. Renee likes to educate people about this invisible syndrome called Fibromyalgia and make people more aware.

What is Fibromyalgia? Try to imagine the last time you had the flu. The aches and pains, stiffness, headaches, feeling drained of energy, unable to get a decent night's sleep, unable to concentrate, discomfort, and at times just a completely unpleasant experience.

Now try to imagine having these flu symptoms all the time, and with all over muscle pain as a permanent constant. This will give you an idea of what it is like to have Fibromyalgia on a good day. Finding a way to manage her Fibromyalgia and improving on her own health and well-being, Renee began her journey toward understanding more about herself and then others. Learning about emotional behaviour and human behaviour, and about the energy that can either help or hinder us, lead Renee to further understanding, but it also made her very sensitive to energy and the energy of others.

This new found sensitivity gave her more clarity and so Renee was able to see more clearly how understanding energy more could help not only herself but others in all areas of their lives. Being this sensitive made it so much easier for Renee to read another person's energy, and learn further about what knowledge they required to achieve their sought after goals.

Also over her many years she has had to live with and manage being diagnosed with severe and sometimes crippling depression. Renee hopes that through her work as a writer, author she would motivate and inspire others to create a life for themselves where they may have once thought there was none due to health or lifestyle issues that they once thought they could not overcome.

Renee also continues her journey of writing as through her work she continues to unmask even more understandings into herself and into other people in aid of helping herself and in hopes of being of some help to other people in need and offer some relief and benefit to those who are seeking further understanding, help and healing.

Through her journey of awareness, understanding emotions, energy, feelings, human behaviour, intuitive energy, transformation and change and more, Renee has gained benefits and healing to help manage her own life and health and she is not done yet as she considers herself a work in progress. Renee believes everyone has something to teach and everyone has something to learn, it does not matter who we are or where we are in life we can all help one another even in some small way, even if it is leading by our own example.

Renee has learnt that whatever is written in a book, be it any book, including this one, that it is only one translation and only one person's opinion, and so Renee writes not to give you something to believe in, but to offer you another point of view so you can go away and form your very own beliefs. There are no beliefs that are completely true and that is why we all continue to search for further answers and understanding and continue to learn and grow and nurture ourselves and our souls in this process.

Renee ask that you please not be offended by any views or writings that you read, and just to remember this is only to provoke awareness and thought, and to provoke further growth of yourself and your soul. This is an opportunity to see life from a different point of view and then create your own views. We are all here to help each other, and we may not agree with one another all the time but at least we can open our minds and then maybe open our hearts to others views so that understanding can be gained and from these understandings, compassion may grow and create a healing that our world so desperately needs.

If you would like to know what is right in your life, or right in this world, you simply have to ask what is hurting yourself or someone else and what is not hurting another. That should give you the path that many should take, and yet so many take the path of hurting another, and no healing can come from this, and it is such a simple message. And have you ever noticed that the questions you may be asking tend to have the simplest of solutions and the simplest of answers.

If parents allowed it children asked many questions and some parents may have thought their child an old soul, not an old soul, the children just asked questions which brought on growth. We have to stop and ask ourselves why we stop asking so many questions. We have to also stop and ask why we decided to stop growing by no longer asking so many questions.

Renee hopes that the understandings that she shares will inspire and motivate a change, a healing and a transformation in others and in our world today.

The Writer wants to be understood much more than he wants to be respected or praised or even loved. And that perhaps, is what makes him different from others. – *Leo C. Rosten*

Live like someone left the gate open!

Introduction

I decided to compile this book due to one day I out of sorts, I open up to Social Media and I read the wisdom that my Social Media friends shared and it gave me a pick me up, that it made me get on with my day with a lot more ease, so I wanted to share that with everyone else and see if it helps another.

I hope that Social Media for the Soul will do the same for you. Also I hope that you will revisit this book, maybe just open the book everyday to gain one quote or a touch of wisdom.

There is so much wisdom out there that we wish we could remember where we saw it or wish we saved it for a rainy day. I hope that this little taste of wisdom and quotes will uplift you as it has done for me.

I hope you find within these pages fun, thought provoking, and when you need it at times maybe a lift when needed.

Thank you for the opportunity to allow me to share a part of what I have come across on my journey and I hope it will enhance your journey as it has done my. I hope you gain as much as I do from these words within these pages.

I do hope that Social Media for the Soul will inspire you to take the time to really read the wisdom that is out there and maybe collect it yourself for your own inspiration or to share with others. I will be waiting.

Thank you for everyone out there in the Social Media World for being there for sharing your wisdom in all its shapes and forms. Thank you for letting me share. Let's keep paying it forward.

Good friends are like stars.

You don't always see them,

but know they're always there.

Watch your thoughts;

They become words;

Watch your words;

They become actions;

Watch your actions;

They become Habits;

Watch your habits;

They become character.

Watch your character;

It becomes your destiny.

Lao Tzu

"To live is the

Rarest thing in the world

Most people just exist.

Oscar Wilde

If we could look into each other's
hearts,

And understand the unique
challenges

Each of us faces. I think we would
treat

Each other much more gently,

With more love, patience,

tolerance and care

Marvin J Ashton.

Sometimes those who don't socialize
Much aren't actually anti-social,
They just have no tolerance for
Drama and fake people.

"Do the best you can
until you know better.
Then when you know better
do better."
Maya Angelou

Listen to yourself in that quietude you
might hear the voice of God.
Maya Angelou final tweet

Sometimes when
Things are falling apart
They may actually
Be falling into place.

Maybe the journey
Isn't so much about
Becoming anything.
Maybe it's about
Un-becoming everything
That isn't really you
So you can be who you
Were meant be
In the first place

> *"One of my main regrets in life is having given considerable thought to inconsiderate people."*

Jarod Kintz

ONE DAY,

Someone will

walk into your

life and make

you see why it

never worked out

with anyone else.

If you are lucky enough

To be different from every else

DON"T CHANGE

Someone who

loves you

wouldn't put

themselves in

a position to

lose you.

Trent Shelton

If someone seriously wants

To be a part of your life,

They will seriously

Make an effort to

Be in it.

No Reasons.

No Excuses.

"If you are always

Trying to be normal

You will never

know

How amazing

you can be"

Maya Angelou

Stop waiting for Friday,

For Summer,

For Some to Fall in Love

With you,

For Retirement,

For Life...

Happiness is achieved when

You stop Waiting for it and

Make something of the

Moment you're in Right Now...

How we treat the vulnerable is how we
define ourselves as a species.

Russell Brand

Faith is a knowledge

within the heart

beyond the reach of proof.

Khail Gibran

Don't Listen

To people who tell You what to do.

Listen to people who encourage you to

Do what you know in

Your heart is right

Nothing ever goes away

Until it teaches

Is what we need to know.

Pema Chodron

Spread seeds of love around wherever you go and with whomever you interact with, and then watch them grow. ~Randi G Fine~

A woman whose
smile is open and
whose expression is
glad has a kind of
Beauty no matter
what she wears.
Anne Roiphe

You are never too old to
Set another goal or to
dream a new dream.
C. S. Lewis

"There is force in the universe,

Which, if we permit it, will flow

Through us and produce

Miraculous results."

Mahatma Gandhi

"All our

dreams can

come true...

if we have

the courage

to pursue

them."

I awoke only to find that the
Rest of the world is still asleep.
Leonardo da Vinci

When you dance
To your own rhythm,
People may not
Understand you; they
May even hate you.
but mostly,
they'll wish
they had the
courage to do
The same.

Your Dream Doesn't
Have An Expiration Date.
Take a Deep Breath,
and Try Again.

I never
make the same mistake twice.
I make it like five or six times,
You know,
Just to be sure

I will thank God for the day
And the moment I have.
Jim Valvano

"The way to get
Started is to quit
Talking and begin
doing."
Walt Disney

Miracles start to happen
When you give as much
energy to your dreams as
you do to your fears.

Life is
a gift.
Wake up
every day
and realize
that.

The world is full
Of magic things,
Patiently waiting
For our senses to
Grow sharper.
Faith is a knowledge
within the heart
beyond the reach of proof.
W. B. Yeats

Who looks outside, dreams;
Who looks inside, awakes.
Carl Jung

"Go confidently
In the direction of your
Dreams.
Live the life you have
Imagined."

Faith is a knowledge
within the heart
beyond the reach of proof.

If you have to keep

wondering where you

stand with someone,

perhaps it's time to stop

standing and start walking.

"Be bold enough
To use your voice,
Brave enough to
Listen to your heart,
And strong
Enough to live the life
You've always imagined
Unknown

Success is liking yourself,
liking what you do,
and liking how you do it.
Maya Angelou

Happiness is not determined
By what's happening around
You but rather what's
Happening inside of you. Most
People depend on others to
gain happiness, but the
truth is, it always comes
from within.

Unknown

Sometimes,
what you're looking
for comes when
you're not
looking at all.

The truth has never denied the Seeker... it is the Seeker who has denied the truth.

Every single thing that has ever happened in your life is preparing you for a moment that is yet to come

Unknown

Girls compete

with each other

women empower

one another.

Where there is desire there

Is gunna be a flame

Where is a flame

Someone's bound to get

Burned but just because it

Burns doesn't mean your

Gunna die you gotta get

Up and

Try Try Try

Pink

It was the sort of bone deep
emotion that made him want
to hold her tighter with one hand,
and draw a sword against the
world with the other

Someone who hates you

Normally hates you for

one of three reasons.

they either see you

as a threat.

They hate themselves.

or they want to be you.

The further a society

Drifts from the truth,

The more it will hate

Those that speak it.

George Orwell

Haters don't really
Hate you
They hate themselves
Because
You're a reflection
of what they
wish to be.

By being
Yourself, you put
Something
Wonderful in the
World that was not
There before."
Edwim Elliot

"A thousand times
We die in one life.
We crumble,
Break and tear
Apart until the
Layers of illusion are
burned away and
all that is left,
is the truth
of who and
what we really are."

Teal Scott

"Whatever we plant in our subconscious

Mind and nourish with repetition and

Emotion will one day become a reality."

Earl Nightingale

You are the universe

The stars, son and

Trees. You are what

Holds the world, you

Are who lives on it.

All is unique yet all

is one.

Sometimes, you find yourself in the
middle of nowhere;
And sometimes, in the middle of
Nowhere,
You find yourself

Have faith the steps
Will appear as you
Walk. Ruthlessly
Surrender all worry.
Nothing is being a
asked it is only
Being offered.

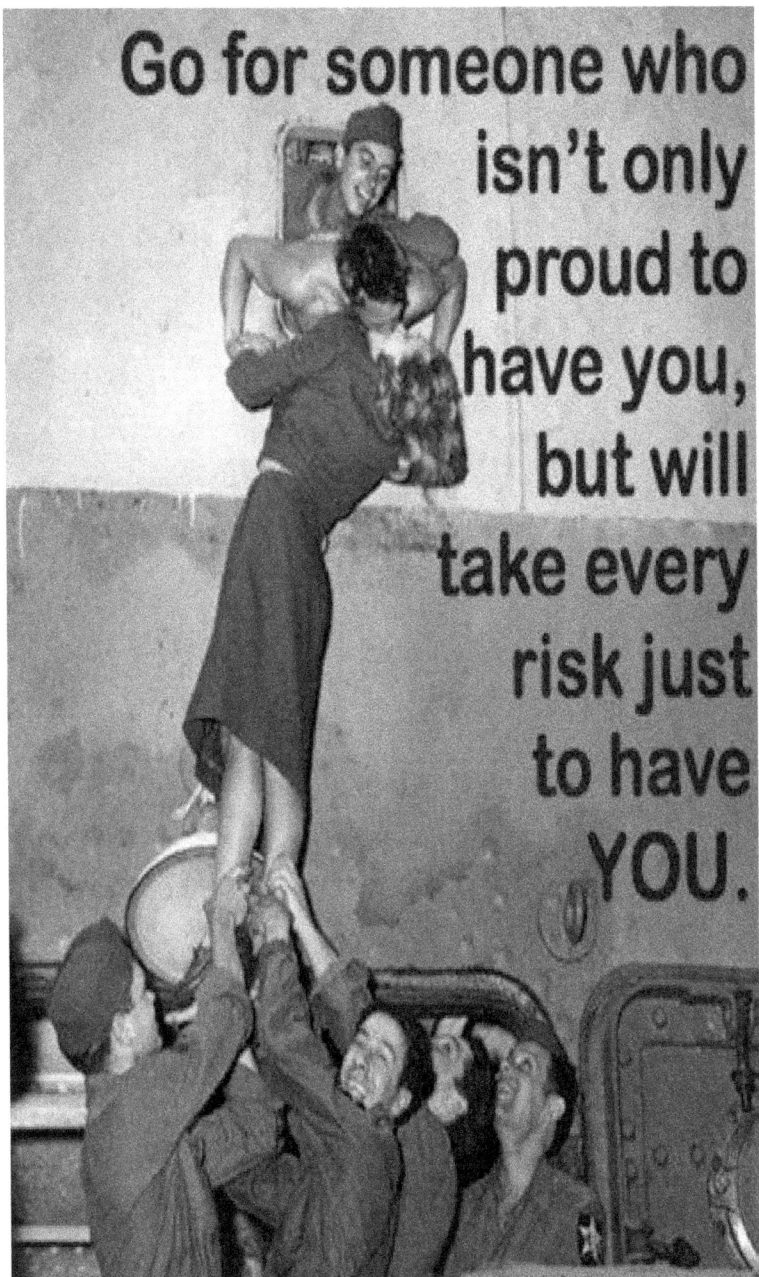

Go for someone who isn't only proud to have you, but will take every risk just to have YOU.

Realize that your world

Is only a reflection

Of yourself

And stop finding fault

With the reflection.

Attend to yourself,

Set yourself right —

Mentally and emotionally

The Physical self

Will follow automatically.

Sri Nisargadatta Maharaj

Rednecks, hippies, misfits – we're all the same Gay or straight? So what? It doesn't matter to me. We have to be concerned about other people, regardless. I don't like seeing anybody treated unfairly. It stick in my craw I hold on to the values from my childhood.

Willie Nelson

Ignoring your Passion

is slow Suicide.

Never ignore what

your heart pumps for.

Mold your career

Around your lifestyle,

Not your lifestyle

Around your career.

A lot of the pain that we are dealing with

are really only THOUGHTS

THE SOUL

USUALLY KNOWS

WHAT TO DO TO

HEAL ITSELF.

THE CHALLENGE

IS TO SILENCE

THE MIND.

Whatever happens,

Where you go,

Whatever you do,

Remember this:

No one can take

The Fire out of your soul,

The Stars

From your eyes,

The Passion

In your heart.

Those are yours

Forever.

S. L

A man sees in the world

What he carries in his heart

Goethe

*At any moment you have a choice
that either leads you closer to your
spirit or further away from it.*

Dear Optimist,

Pessimist, and Realist,

*While you guys were busy arguing
about the glass of water,*

I drank it.

Sincerely,

The Opportunist.

I think a hero

Is any person

Really intent

On making this

a better place

For all people

Maya Angelou

Understand that you own nothing,
Everything that surrounds you is
temporary, only the love in your heart
will last forever.

IF YOU EVER FALL IN LOVE...

Fall in love with someone who wants to know your favourite colour and just how you like your coffee. Fall in love with someone who loves the way you laugh and would do absolutely anything to hear it. Fall in love with someone who puts their head on your chest just to hear your heart beat.

Fall in love with someone who kisses you in public and is proud to show you off to anyone they know. Fall in love with someone who would never ever want to hurt you. Fall in love with someone who falls in love with your flaws and thinks you are perfect just the way you are. Fall in love with someone who thinks that you are the **ONE** *they would love to wake up to each day.*

*Don't be in such
a hurry to condemn a
person because he
doesn't do what you
do, or think as you
think. There was a
time when you didn't
know what you know
today*

Malcolm X

*Practicing forgiveness does not
Mean accepting wrong doing."*

If you want to live a
Happy life, tie it to a goal,
Not to people or objects.
Albert Einstein

Kindness is
Not an act. It
Is a lifestyle.
Anthony Douglas

On earth the soul is
Invisible and it's hard
To believe in what you
Can't see

Unexpected blessings arise
From determined patience.

If someone thinks that
Love and peace is a cliché
That must have been left
Behind in the Sixties.
That's his problem.
Love and peace
Are eternal.

John Lennon

Never hate people

Who are jealous of you, but
Respect their jealously. They're
People who think that you're
Better than them.

Dream with
Your heart
And love with
Your soul

The most common way people

Give up their power is by

Thinking they don't

Have any.

Alice Walker

"Absorb what is useful,

Discard what is not. Add what is
uniquely your own."

Bruce Lee

I think hell is something

You carry around with you.

Not somewhere you go.

Neil Gaiman

12 Steps for Self Care

1. *If it feels wrong, don't do it.*
2. *Say "exactly" what you mean.*
3. *Don't be a people pleaser.*
4. *Trust your instincts.*
5. *Never speak badly about yourself.*
6. *Never give up on your dreams.*
7. *Don't be afraid to say "No".*
8. *Don't be afraid to say "Yes"*
9. *Be* **KIND** *to yourself.*
10. *Let go of what you can't control.*
11. *Stay away from drama and negativity.*
12. **LOVE**

Let's try
teaching children
How
to think
instead of
What
To think.

Detachment is not that
You should own nothing.
But that nothing
Should own you.
Ali Ibn Ani Talib

Stand up

For what you

Believe

in.

Even if

It means

Standing alone.

If you are not doing what you love,

You are wasting your time.

Billy Joel

Most people do not
Really want freedom,
Because freedom
Involves responsibility,
And most people are
Frightened of
Responsibility...

People who uplift you are
The best kind of people.
You don't simply keep
Them. You have to
Treasure them.

Dodinsky

The pursuit, even of the best things
Ought to be calm and tranquil.
Marcus Tullius Cicero

Take time today to
Rest and retreat.
Honour your sensitivity
By avoiding harsh or
Intense situations
As much as possible.

You can easily judge

The character of a man

By how he treats those

Who can do nothing for him.

James D. Miles

Attitude is a little thing that makes

A big difference.

Author Unknown

There is a huge

Amount of

Freedom that

Comes to you

When you take

Nothing Personally.

Don Miguel Ruiz

It's a Journey...No one is ahead of

you or behind you. You are not more

"advanced" or less enlightened. You

are exactly where you need to be. It's

Not a Contest....

It's LIFE. *We are* ALL *teachers and we*

are all students.

some see
a weed,

some see
a wish.

If you want to awaken all of humanity, then awaken all of yourself. If you want to eliminate all that is dark and negative in yourself. Truly, the greatest gift you have to give is that of your own self transformation.

Lao Tzu

"Unexpressed

emotions will never

die. They are

buried alive and

will come forth

later in uglier ways."

Sigmund Freud

To the mind that is still, the
whole universe surrenders.
Lao Tzu

Forces of light on earth
shall overcome the forces of darkness.
Complete spiritual enlightenment on
earth will occur.
Edgar Cayce

If light is in your heart,
You will find your way home.
Rumi

There comes a time in life, when you way away from all the drama and people who create it. Surround yourself with people who make your laugh, forget the bad, and focus on the good. Love the people who treat you right. Pray for the ones who don't. Life is too short to be anything but happy. Falling down is part of life, getting back up is living.

*I cannot learn
other people's lessons
for them. They must
do the work
themselves, and
they will do it
when they are
ready.*

*The warrior who trusts his path
doesn't need to prove
the other is wrong.*

Paulo Coelho

Anger cannot be overcome
By anger. If someone is
Angry with you, and you
Show anger in return, the
Result is a disaster. On the
Other hand, if you control
Your anger and show its
Opposite – love, compassion,
Tolerance and patience – not
only will you remain
Peaceful, but the other
Person's anger will also diminish.

Dalai Lama

"Looking behind I am filled
with gratitude. Looking
forward I am filled with vision.
Looking upwards I am filled
with strength. Looking within
I discover peace."

Q'ero Indians

Live as if you were to die tomorrow.
Learn as if you were to live forever

Mahatma Gandhi

Don't confuse your path with
your destination. Just because
it's stormy now doesn't mean that
you aren't headed for sunshine.
Unknown

Free yourself from the limitations
Others have placed on you
And your world will transform

The greatest danger for most of us is
not that our aim is too high and we
miss it, but that our aim is too
low and we hit it.

When she says that she loves you,
know that she loves you more
than you'll ever understand.

Holding on to anger is like drinking poison and expecting the other person to die.

Buddha

Wisdom is often times nearer when we stoop than when we soar.

William Wordsworth

Life only comes around once, so do whatever makes you happy, and be with whoever makes you smile.

Every time you put something positive into the universe, the world changes. Your kindness invites miracles to show up. Not just in your world but in the whole world.

Don't dance around the perimeter of the person you want to be step in fully and completely.

Stop rehearsing life's failures.

Use your beautiful imagination

to visualize success.

Cheryl Richardson

Don't carry your mistakes around with you. Instead, place them under your feet and use them as stepping stones. Never regret. If it's good, it's wonderful. If it's bad, it's experience.

"ALL THAT WE ARE

IS A RESULT OF ALL THAT WE

THOUGHT."

BUDDHA

We all have
a beautiful light within...
We just sometimes forget it is there.
John Holland

Spend your time with
people who only want the
very best for you.
And be someone who only
wants the very best for
others, too.
Cheryl Richardson

If you are depressed

*you are live living in the **past**.*

If you are anxious

*you are living in the **future***

If you are at peace,

you are living in the present.

Lao Tzu

I love people who make me laugh. I honestly think it's the thing I like most, to laugh. It cures a multitude of ills. It's probably the most important thing in a person.

Audrey Hepburn

*Begin at once to live, and count each
separate day as a separate life.*

Seneca

I just woke up one day

and decided I didn't want

to feel like that anymore,

or ever again.

So I changed.

It might take a year,

It might take a day, but

What's meant to be will

always find it way.

*Be less curious
about people
and
more curious about ideas.*

Marie Curie

*Real knowledge
is to know the extent
of one's ignorance.*

Confucius

*A new attitude invariably
creates a new result.*

You can be the moon and still be jealous of the stars.

Gary Allan

Your worst

enemy cannot

harm you

as much as

your own

unguarded

thoughts.

Buddha

"You must learn to get in touch with the innermost essence of your Being. This true essence is beyond the ego. It is fearless; it is free; it is immune to criticism; it does not fear any challenge. It is beneath no one, superior to no one, and full of magic, mystery, and enchantment."

Deepak Chopra

Giving up
on your goal
because of
one setback
is like
slashing
your other
three Tires
because
you got a Flat.
Christine Kane

Everyone is gifted but some people
never open their packages.

The authentic self will come through when you're no longer performing, pretending, or denying – when you are true to yourself. Being authentic is a moment to moment proposition. It's a never-ending journey.

"Perhaps the butterfly is proof that you can go through a great deal of darkness yet become something beautiful."

Humble enough to

know I'm not

better than

anybody

& wise enough

to know that I'm

different from the

rest.

Those who don't believe in

magic will never find it.

Roald Dahl

When the power of love overcomes the love of power the world will know peace.

Jimi Hendrix

Small opportunities are often the beginning of great achievement.

When you feel like QUITTING *think about why you* STARTED

I AM.

*Two of the
most powerful
words; for
what you put
after them
shapes your
reality.*

*When the realization is deep,
your whole Being is Dancing.*

Nature does

not hurry,

yet everything is

ACCOMPLISHED.

Lao Tzu

You must find the place

inside yourself where

nothing is impossible.

Many of the obstacles

you once imagined are

not even there.

LOVE

YOURSELF

FOR ALL

YOU HAVE BEEN

ALL YOU ARE

AND ALL

YOU WILL

BECOME.

"Being honest may not get you many friends but it'll always get you the rights ones."

John Lennon

What is to give light must

endure burning.

Viktor E. Frankl

A Woman in harmony with her
Spirit

is like a river flowing.

She goes where she will without

pretence and arrives at her

destination prepared to be herself

and only herself.

Maya Angelou

You never know how strong
you are till being strong is
the only choice you have.
Bob Marley

All that we see of seem is
but a dream within a dream
Edgar Allan Poe

"Happiness is when
what you think
what you say
and what you do
are in Harmony.

"If you always put limits on everything you do, physical or anything else, it will spread into your work and into your life, there are no limits. There are only plateaus, and you must not stay there, you must go Beyond them.
Bruce Lee

"There are
people in your
life whom you
unknowingly
inspire simply
by being you.

You have to
understand , most of
these people are not
ready to be
unplugged. And many
of them are so inert,
so hopelessly
dependent on the
system that they will
fight to protect it.

Anger Clouds the Mind
Hatred Blurs the Vision
Peace Clears the Mind
Love Restores the Vision.

Today is your day to
let go of things
that no longer
serve you.

May you be at peace,
May your hear remain open,
May you awaken to the light
of your own true nature,
May you be healed,
May you be a source of
Healing for all Beings.

Everyone thinks of changing the world, but no one thinks of changing themselves.

Truth is so obscure in these times, and falsehood so established, that, unless we love the Truth, we cannot know it.

Blaise Pascal

The door to wisdom is

knowing yourself.

"THE MORE SCARED

WE ARE OF A WORK OR CALLING,

THE MORE SURE

WE CAN BE THAT

WE ACTUALLY HAVE TO DO IT."

Steven Pressfield

A teacher is never a give of truth;

He is a guide, a pointer to the

truth that each student

must find for himself.

Bruce Lee

"Don't just teach your children
to read... teach them to
question what they read.
Teach them to question
everything.
George Carlin

Some people

come into your life as

BLESSINGS

others come in your life as

LESSONS...

"Energy,

like you,

has no beginning

and no end.

It can never be

destroyed.

It is only ever

shifting states."

Panache Desai

Don't follow

my footsteps.

I run into walls.

"When I was 5 years old, my mother always told me that happiness was the key to life. When I went to school, they asked me what I wanted to be when I grew up. I wrote down 'happy'. They told me I didn't understand the assignment, and I told them they didn't understand life.

John Lennon

If you can't get rid of the

skeleton in your closet

you'd best teach it to

dance.

George Bernard Shaw

If you share your dreams with a
small dreamer, they can sometimes
rain on your parade.

Keep your faith and just jump
in the puddles.

"Many people, especially, ignorant people, want to punish you for speaking the truth for being correct, for being you.

Never apologize for being correct, or for being years ahead of your time.

If you're right and you know it, speak your mind. Even if you are a minority of one, the truth is still the truth.'

Gandhi

The body is constantly 'in process'.

Stillness is impossible. It is active.

It is a field of frequency operating

within a field of frequency.

All vibes serve wellness.

I cannot tell you any
spiritual truth that
deep within you don't
know already. All I can
do is remind you of what
you have forgotten.
Eckhart Tolle

You are destined for
Greatness.
Just keep walking
you are
almost there!

Education Is Not The Learning
Of Facts, But The Training
Of The Mind To Think.

Albert Einstein

It's about being
alive and feisty
and not sitting down
and shutting up
even when people
would like you to.

Pink

Out of suffering

have emerged

the strongest

souls; the most

massive characters are

seared with scars.

You are a beautiful creation,

perfectly imperfect... a work in progress... you have everything you need to fulfil your purpose... don't dilute yourself for any person or any reason... you are enough... be unapologetically you.

Dr. Steve Maraboli

"*You cannot solve a problem from the same consciousness that created it. You must learn to see the world anew.*

Albert Einstein

People Don't
Need To Be
Saved Or
Rescued.
People Need
Knowledge
Of Their Own
Power And
How To
Access It.

Give freely,
love fully,
and play feverously!
Don't put so many
conditioned rules
on your happiness.
Life can be a
Beautiful
experience if
we allow it.

Dr. Steve Maraboli

"Instead of getting even or teaching someone a lesson when they do you wrong, consider teaching yourself a lesson instead. Revenge keeps you psychically connected to another in a negative way. Release yourself through the liberating act of forgiveness, and learn a truly valuable spiritual lesson."

Sri Gawn Tu Fahr

Journey into your own heart...
What you seek
has always
been within.

There will always be a reason
why you meet people.
Either you need them to
change your life or you're the
one who will change theirs.

My wish for you is
that you continue.
Continue to be
who and how you
are, to astonish a
mean world with
your acts of
kindness. Continue
to allow humor to
lighten the burden
of your tender
heart.

Maya Angelou

"It is curious that physical courage should be so common in the world and moral courage so rare."

EVERYTHING IS CONNECTED...

The most important kind of freedom is to be who you really are.
Jim Morrison

*The Strongest
people are not
those who show
strength in front
of us but those who
win battles we
know nothing
about.*

*I want every little girl who is told
she is bossy to be told she has
leadership skills.*
Sheryl Sandberg

Every great dream

begins with a dreamer/

Always remember,

you have within you

the strength, the patience

and the passion

to reach for the stars

to change the world.

Patience is the best remedy

for every trouble.

Plautus

"Today is a new day! Don't let your history interfere with your destiny. It doesn't matter what you did or where you were... it matters where you are and what you're doing. Get out there! Sing the song in your heart and **NEVER** let anyone shut you up!"

Dr. Steve Maraboli

You will only being to heal when you let go of past hurts, forgive those who have wronged you and learn to forgive yourself for your mistakes

"*Believe nothing. No matter where you read it, or who said it. No matter if I have said it. Unless it agrees with your own reason and your own common sense.*"

Buddha

You unlock the door to greater Levels of excellence and success When you accept who you are. It is from this point of acceptance that we can create a masterful life.

Dr. Steve Maraboli

No one is born hating another person because of the colour of his skin, of his background or his religion. People learn to hate, and if they can learn to hate, they can be taught to love, for love comes more naturally to the human heart than it's opposite.

Nelson Mandela

There is nothing
more beautiful
that the way
the ocean refuses
to stop kissing the shoreline
no matter how many times
it is sent away.
Sarah Kay

I can't change you or how
you treat me, but I can
leave you
and realize that I am worth
much more that you could
ever give me.

The opinion which

other people have of you

is their problem,

not yours.

Elisabeth Kubler-Ross

It is not a question

of being in Love

with someone.

It is a question

Of being Love.

Osho

As near as I can
tell they're fighting
over which religion
is the most peaceful!

It is a great injustice, and a
monumental act of cruelty
for any religion to make
someone fear God.
Hafiz

"Don't lose your passion
or the fighter that's
inside of you."
Pink

"Body confidence
is when you
honour your body for
being the home to an
incredible soul."
Jessica Ortner

"Love is what we are in our essence
and the more love we feel in our
hearts. The more it will be
brought to us.
Deepak Chopra

BE
Unapologetically
YOU

Steve Maraboli

It's not always about sex.

sometimes the best type of intimacy

is where you just lay back, laugh

together at the stupidest things,

hold each other, and enjoy each

other's company.

A Shift in

perspective makes

the particles in your

universe dance to

new possibilities.

Let yourself be silently drawn

by the strange pull

of what you really love,

it will not lead you astray.

Rumi

The truth you
believe and
cling to,
makes you
unavailable
to hear
anything new.
Pema Chodron

'Set your life
on fire.
Seek those
who fan
your flames.
Rumi

Your task is not to seek for love,

but merely to seek and find

all the barriers within yourself

that you have built against it.

Rumi

"It takes courage... to

endure the sharp pains of

self – discovery, rather than

choose to take the dull pain

of unconsciousness that

would last the rest of our

lives.

Marrianne Williamson

Life is a school, where you learn how to remember what your soul already knows.

Your vision will become clear only when you can look into your own heart

Carl Jung

When the mind is pure, joy follows like a shadow that never leaves.

Buddha

"This is my simple religion. There is no need for temple; no need for complicated philosophy. Our own brain, our own heart is out temple; the philosophy is kindness.

Dalai Lama

When you get down

to the heart

of the matter

the heart

is

what matters.

You can't play it safe your whole life and expect to reach your highest potential. You've got to be willing to take some risk.

J. Osteen

The soul always knows what to do to heal itself. The challenge is to silence the mind.

Strong people don't put others down they life them up.

*Trust your
inner voice
to guide you.
It's better than any* **GPS**
and doesn't cost a thing!

When you focus on
PROBLEMS
*You will have more
Problems.
When you focus on*
POSSIBILITIES
*you'll have more
opportunities.*

Anticipate the difficult by managing the easy.
Lao Tzu

The secret of getting ahead is getting started.
Mark Twain

One of the happiest moments ever is when you find the courage to let go of what you can't change.

FORGIVENESS *is the most powerful thing you can do for yourself on the spiritual path. If you can't learn to forgive, you can forget about getting to higher levels of awareness.*

Affirm: I forgive everyone, including myself.

Wayne Dyer

Those who are the hardest

to Love

need it the most.

Who is richest

is content with the least,

for content is wealth of nature.

Socrates

Life isn't about

waiting for

the storm

to pass it's about

learning to dance in the rain.

"You cannot get through
a single day without having an
impact on the world around you.
What you do makes a difference and
you have to decide what kind of
difference you want to make.
Jane Goodall

In order for
you to insult
me, I would
first have to
value your
opinion.
Unknown

Live your life
take chances
be crazy.
Don't wait.
Because right now
is the oldest
you've ever been
and the youngest
you'll be ever again.

To make a difference in someone's life
you don't have to be brilliant, rich
beautiful, or perfect. You just have
to care enough and be there.

*Never let
the sadness
of your past
and the fear
of your future
ruin the
happiness of
your present.*

*People inspire you,
or they drain you.
Choose Wisely.*

Do not let

the waves of

DOUBT

Wash away

Your authentic self.

Bravery

is believing in

Yourself.

Stop keeping track of the mistakes

you've made – it's time

to forgive yourself.

I may not be the most

important

person in your life.

I just hope that when you

hear my name

you smile and say

That's My Friend!

"Be a rainbow

in someone else's cloud.

Maya Angelou

Here's to all the people
who get back up more times
than they are knocked down,
who give more than they ever
expect to receive,
Who still show love to others,
even when their own heart is broken,
Who smile through the sad times,
who light the way for others,
Who spread laughter and joy.
Thank you for making the
world a better place.

"All that we are is the result of what we have thought."
Think Love, Be Love.
Buddha

Sending loving thoughts to all who feel hurt or alone today. I may not be able to take your hurt away, but I can let you know I care.

Silence is a source of great strength.
Lao Tzu

Be true to yourself.

Don't let other people decide
what you should do, or what is
best for you, or who they think
that you should be. You only have
one life, choose your own path.

Just be you!

We would do
ourselves a
tremendous favour
by letting go of the people
who poison our spirit.

Dr. Steve Maraboli

What Doesn't
Kill You
Make You

~~Cranky~~

~~Stronger~~

~~Pissed Off~~

~~Stronger~~

~~Grumpy~~

Stronger

(It may take a whole

But you'll get there!)

Can we start the

weekend over?

I wasn't ready!

Seek the magic in

life and suddenly

the ordinary

becomes

extraordinary.

Don't pray for an easier life.

Pray to be stronger instead.

John F. Kennedy

"The best
way to
predict the
future is to
create it."

Love me without fear.
Trust me without questioning.
Need me without demanding.
Want me without restrictions
Accept me without change.
Desire me without limitations.
For a love so free
will never fly away.

At the end of the
day, the only
questions I will
ask myself are...
Did I Love enough?
Did I laugh
enough?
Did I make a
differences?

Inner peace begins in the moment
you choose not to allow another
person or event to control your
emotions.
Unknown Author

No matter how many mistakes you make or how slow you progress, you are still way ahead of everyone who isn't trying.
Unknown

Optimism is the faith that leads to achievement. Nothing can be done without hope or confidence.
Helen Kelller

"Spread love everywhere you go:

First of all in your own house...

let no one ever come to you

without leaving better and happier.

Be the living expression of God's kindness;

kindness in your face

Kindness in your eyes

Kindness in your smile.

Mother Teresa

"We must be open to our mistakes and grow. Growth isn't based on being perfect, but moving toward the best we can be by being honest."
Tsem Tulku Rinpoche

Why Worry?
If you've done the very best you can, worrying won't make it any better
Walt Disney

Forgive others, not because
they deserve forgiveness,
but because you deserve peace.

Happiness does not depend
on what you have or
who you are.
It solely relies on
what you think?
Buddha

When men are oppressed.
It's a Tragedy,
When women are oppressed,
it Tradition.

"*Walk away from anything or anyone who takes away from your joy. Life is too short to put up with fools.*"

Unknown

Sometimes you need to distance yourself to see things clearly.

Unknown

"You are what you are because it's what you have chosen to be.
If your unhappy
You Must Change
From The Inside
Out.
Steve Maraboli

IMPOSSIBLE

Is not a fact. It is an
Opinion

Hate one; prolong suffering.

Love all: rejoice in happiness.

Such is human

psychology

that if we don't

express our

joy,

we soon cease

to feel it.

Lin Yutang

Smiling is definitely one
of the best beauty
remedies.
If you have a good senses
Of humour and a good
approach to life
that's beautiful.
Rashida Jones

Only the weak are cruel. Gentleness
can only be expected from the strong.
Leo Buscaglia

"When you think
everything is
someone else's fault,
you will suffer a lot."
Dalai Lama

Everything you can imagine is real.
Pablo Picasso

"It's not
whether you
get knocked
down, it's whether
you get back up."
Vince Lombardi (NFL Coach)

The most
sophisticated
people I know
inside they are
all children.

Growth is
Change is
Painful
but nothing is
as painful as
staying stuck
somewhere
you don't belong.
Mandy Hale

Jealousy comes from counting others blessings instead of your own.

Unknown

Opportunity is missed by most people because it is dressed in overalls and looks like work.

Thomas A. Edison

It is not in the stars to hold our destiny but in ourselves.
William Shakespeare

If you don't like where you are Change It you're not a Tree.

The truth is like a lion. You don't have to defend it. Let it loose. It will defend itself.

The most painful thing
is losing yourself in the
process
of loving someone too much
and forgetting that you are
special too.
Unknown

"A good traveller has no fixed plans,
and is not intend on arriving."
Lao Tzu

Three things cannot be long hidden:
the sun, the moon, and the truth.
Buddha

"Do not allow
yourself to be
damaged by
yourself."
Steve Maraboli

"Sometimes you put walls up
not to keep people out,
but to see who care enough
to break them down."
Socrates

Well life has a funny way

of sneaking up on you

when you think

everything's okay and

everything's going right

and life has a funny way

of helping you out

when You think everything's

gone wrong and

everything blows up

in your face.

Alanis Morissette

"Birds born in a
cage think flying
is an illness."
Alejandro Jodorowski

We must let go of the life we have
planned, so as to accept
the one that is waiting for us.
Joseph Campbell

I can't o back to yesterday
because I was a different person then.

Psychologist say, once you learn how to be happy you won't tolerate being around people who make you feel anything less.

If a person want to be a part
of your life,
they will make an obvious effort to
do so.
Think twice before reserving a
space in your heart
for people who do not make an
effort to stay.
Unknown

Cuddling literally kills
depression, relieves
anxiety and strengthens
the immune system.

There are no mistakes.
no coincidences.
All events are blessings
given to us to learn from.
Eliaabeth Kubler-Ross

Let yourself be silently drawn by the
strange pul of what you really love.

It will not lead you astray.
Rumi

"When arise in the morning, think of what a precious privilege it is to be alive – to breathe, to think, to enjoy, to love.

Marcus Aurelius

"I am so grateful for my troubles. As I reflect back on my life. I have come to realize that my greatest triumphs have been born of my greatest troubles."

Steve Maraboli

It takes a great

deal of courage

to see the world

in all its tainted

glory, and still

to love it.

Oscar Wilde

The pure and simple truth is rarely

pure and never simple.

Oscar Wilde

While you're busy looking for the perfect person, you'll probably miss the imperfect person who could make you perfectly happy.

Unknown

Don't allow yourself to wake up with yesterday's issues troubling your mind. Refuse to life backwards, see every day as a new chapter.

No one is useless
in this world
who lightens
the burden of it
for somebody else
Charles Dickens

"Too many of use
are not living
our dreams
because we are
living our fears."
Les Brown

People don't always need advice.
Sometimes all they really need is a
hand to hold
an earn to listen, and a heart to
understand them.

Every person from your past
lives as a shadow in your mind.
Good or bad, they all helped you
write the story of your life, and
shaped the person you are today.
Doe Zantamata

If you really want to do something you'll find a way. If you don't you'll find an excuse.

Unknown

If your life isn't going the way you want, it's time you start hanging out with your future and stop hanging out with your past.

"The
empowered
woman is
powerful beyond
measure and
beautiful beyond
description.
Steve Maraboli

I shall continue to do
what is right
whether
anybody likes it or not.
Harry S Truman

Heartbreaking image by an Iraqi artist taken in an orphanage. This little girl has never seen her mother, so she drew a mom on the ground and fell asleep with her.

"Appreciate what you have, since you don't know what you've got until it's taken away from you... That's when it is too late."

*""You can't get much
done in life if you
only work on the
days when you feel
good."*
**Jerry West
(Retired LA Lakers NBA Champion)**

*When there is
no enemy within,
the enemies outside
cannot hurt you.*
African proverb

Just don't give up
trying to do
what you really
want to.
Ella Fitzgerald

To be wronged is nothing unless you
continue to remember it.
Confucius

Coincidence is God's way
of remaining anonymous.
Albert Einstein

You have to
Love me for
WHO I AM
and not what
you would like
me to BE.

It is easier to build
up a child
than it is to
repair an adult
choose your words wisely.

I have no time to "Hate People"

Who "Hate Me"

Because

I am busy "Loving People"

Who "Love Me."

Burn the candles, use

the nice sheets, wear

the fancy lingerie. Don't

save it for a special

occasion today is

special.

Unknown

"Who are you to judge
the life I live?
I am not perfect and I
don't have to be!
Before you start pointing
fingers, make sure your
hands are clean."
Bob Marley

There's a story behind every person,
a reason why they are the way they
are so, think about that before
you judge someone

"Learn from

your history

but don't

live in it.

Steve Maraboli

Be kind

to unkind

people.

They need it

he most.

"Happiness is not in
the mere possession
of money.
It lies in the joy of
achievement,
in the thrill of creative
effort."
Franklin D. Roosevelt

Souls recognize
each other by the way
they feel not by
the way they look.

When one door of

happiness closes,

another opens,

but often we look

so long at the closed door

that we do not see

the one that has been

opened for us.

'You were created to be completely

loved and completely lovable

for your whole life'

Deepak Chopra

I've learned that people will forget what you said, people will forget what you did, but people will never forget how you made them feel.

Maya Angelou

You Can't start the next chapter of your life if you keep re-reading your last one.

Unknown

When something bas happens, you can either let it define you let it destroy you or let it strengthen you. The choice is yours.

Unknown

I don't engage in acts of kindness to be rewarded later, I engage in acts of kindness because it makes me feel Good to Give.

Never allow
loneliness to drive
you back into the
arms of someone
you know you
don't belong with.

Your dream doesn't
have an expiration date
take a deep breath, and try again.

"Anyone who stops
learning is old, whether
at twenty or eighty.
Anyone who keeps
learning stays young.
The greatest thing in
life is to keep your
mind young."
Henry Ford

Never underestimate the power that is,
And has always been within you.
Melanie Moushigian Koulouris

How I feel when my favorite song comes on

The universe does not know the difference between past, present or future. It is responding to your current feeling and delivering you more of the same.

An arrow can only be shot by pulling it backward. So when life is dragging you back with difficulties. It means that it's going to launch you into something great. So just focus, and keep aiming.

Rather

than being your

thoughts and emotions

be

the awareness

behind them.

Eckhart Tolle

Love is the key

to your spiritual growth

love is the key

to the world's spiritual evolution.

"You need to learn how to select our thoughts just the same way you select your clothes every day. This is a power you can cultivate"

Elizabeth Gilbert

Eat, Pray, Love

Sometimes a perfect memory can be ruined if put to words.

Nova Ren Suma

Let go of the people
who dull your shine,
poison your spirit,
and bring you drama
Cancel your subscription to their issues.

Dr. Steve Maraboli

The way to get started is to quit talking and begin doing.

Walt Disney

Don't forget that you're human. It's okay to have a melt down. Just don't unpack and live there. Cry it our and then refocus on where you are headed.

Our capacity to make peace with another person and with the world depends very much on our capacity to make peace with ourselves.

Thich Nhat Hanh

Life will break you. Nobody can protect you from that, and living alone won't either, for solitude will also break you with its yearning. You have to love. You have to feel. It is the reason you are here on earth. You are here to risk your heart. You are here to be swallowed up. And when it happens that you are broken, or betrayed, or left, or hurt, or death brushes near, let yourself sit by an apple tree and listen to the apples falling all around you in heaps, wasting their sweetness. Tell yourself you tasted as many as you could.

Louise Erdrich

*Our true beauty
comes from within.
We are all unique
flowers blossoming
in our
own special way!*

*No matter what you
two are going through,
treat each other with
respect.*

To be of service

to Spirit

is a blessing

beyond all words.

John Roger

Life is an echo.

what you send out

comes back.

What you sow you reap.

What you give you get.

What you see in others

Exists in you.

" *What you are is a complicated girl with simple needs. You need your books and time to read, and you need a few friends and you need someone-not to take care of you, but to care for you. If you have all those things, you'll always be alright.*"

The most

attractive thing

anyone can do is

exactly what they

said they were

going to do.

Listen to the passion of

your soul, set the wings

of your spirit free and

let not a single song

so unsung.

Sylvana Rossetti

Sometimes you can't explain what you see in a person it's just the way they take you to a place where no one else can.

Man is free the Moment he wishes To be.

Voltaire

If I let

you in,

please

don't

break

anything.

I AM *without form, without limit*

beyond space, beyond time, **I AM**

everything, everything is in me, **I AM**

the Bliss of the Universe

Everywhere **I AM.**

Swani Rama Tirha

Love isn't all about flirting, hugs, kissing and sex. Love is about having the ability to take all those things away and still have feelings for that person.

When did I know I was in love? I knew it the moment I realize that even the smallest room seemed so vastly empty when she was not near me.

Steve Maraboli

If life
can remove
someone
you never
dreamed of
losing, it can
replace them
with someone
you never
dreamt of
having.

Live so that
all your acts
are acts
of kindness.

"There are souls
in this world which
have the gift of
finding joy
everywhere and
of leaving it behind
them when they go."
Frederick Faber

I like people with depth, I like people with emotion, I like people with a strong mind, an interesting mind, a twisted mind, and also people that can make me smile.

Abbey Lee Kershaw

BY BEING YOURSELF *you put something wonderful in the world that was not there before.*

Within each of us, there is silence.

A silence as vast as the universe.

And when we experience that silence,

we remember who we are.

It is a risk to love.

What if it doesn't work out?

Ah, but what if it does.

Peter McWilliams

Trust the wisdom of your soul

It knows the way.

"When you find someone
Who breaks you open and
Makes you feel things;
You fight for them."
Tarryn Fisher

Silence is one of the great
arts of conversation.
Marcus Tullius Cicero

When you do what you love –
You automatically affect
The world around you
In positive ways

It's bad manners
to say *"I love you"*
With a mouth full of

LIES.

You and I are the force for transformation in the world. We are the consciousness that will define the nature of the reality as we are moving into.

Ram Dass

Unless it's mad, passionate, extraordinary love, it's a waste of your time. There are too many mediocre things in life. Love shouldn't be one of them.

Express your love
in everything
you do, think and say.

Be who you are and say what you
feel, because those who mind don't
matter. And those who matter
don't mind.
Bernard M. Baruch

"It's easy to
take off your
clothes and
have sex.
People do it
all the time,
but Opening
up your Soul
to someone,
letting them
into your
spirit, thoughts,
fears, hopes, dreams....
that is being

NAKED

To be love in the world

You must be love

in your own

Heart.

There are many

things in life

that will

catch your eyes,

but only a

few will

catch your

Hearts....

pursue those.

"Learn how to see.
Realize that everything connects to
everything else."
Leonardo da Vinci

All that spirits desire,
Spirits attain.
Khalil Gibran

Every morning we are born again.
What we do today is what
matters most.
Buddha

Never allow your happiness to depend on a relationship. I think it's a very special thing to find love. It's beautiful. Nothing can match it. But make sure you find other things in life that you love besides... your love.

Be with someone who brings out the best in you, not the stress in you.

I travelled the world for decades, seeking wisdom and spiritual knowledge.
But at the end of the journey. I found that it was in my heart all along.
Denise Linn

We have come into this exquisite world to experience ever and ever more deeply our divine courage, freedom and light!
Hafiz

Don't force a relationship that doesn't fit. Your life naturally makes room for the people who are meant to be there.

We gain the strength of the temptation we resist.
Ralph Waldo Emerson

Love does hurt. Loving the wrong person does.

*You have to learn
to get up from the table
when love is no longer
being served.*

*I don't want a
lukewarm love.
I want it to burn
my lips and
engulf my soul.*
Woori

It helps if you remember that everyone is doing their best from their level of consciousness.

-Deepak Chopra

There is no remedy for love

but to love more.

Henry David Thoreau

I may not be your first date, your

first kiss, or your first love, and

that's find, because I just want to

be your last.

It's easy to show skin.

It takes bravery to show

humility, vulnerability,

- compassion, heart, -

kindness, & self-respect.

Mandy Hale

YOU WANT TO BE
A PART OF MY LIFE,
THE DOOR IS
ALWAYS OPEN.
YOU WANT TO
LEAVE MY LIFE,
THE DOOR IS OPEN.
BUT DON'T STAND
AT THE DOOR,
YOU'RE BLOCKING
THE TRAFFIC.

A good woman
doesn't want
perfect, she wants
honesty and
someone who is
man enough to
realize that she
deserves the truth.

Hand in hand together, we
claim our right of birth, and rise
above divisions as people of the Earth.

The wrong
relationships
teach you
how to
recognize the
right one
when it arrives.
~Mandy Hale

"There is no such thing
as a simple act of
compassion or an
inconsequential act of
service.Everything we do
for another person has
infinite consequences."

Caroline Myss

Respect is earned.
Honesty is appreciated.
Trust is gained. Loyalty
is returned.

An Intelligent man
will open your mind.

A Handsome man will
open your eyes.

A Gentleman will
Open your heart.

I am not a one in a

million kind of girl.

I'm a once in a

lifetime kind of

WOMAN

Give me the wisdom

to know what

must be done and the

courage to do it.

We often forget that we are nature.
Nature is not something separate
from us. So when we say that we
have lost our connection to nature,
we've lost our connection to ourselves.

~Andy Goldsworthy

YOUR WORST

BATTLE IS

BETWEEN WHAT

YOU KNOW AND

WHAT YOU FEEL.

*nothing haunts us
like the things
we don't say*

Peace comes from within.

Do not seek it without.

Buddha

Honesty is

the highest

form of intimacy

Stop worrying

about what can

go wrong. And

get excited about

what can go right.

Awareness is like the sun.
When it shines on things
they are transformed.
Thich Nhat Hanh

Sometimes all you need
is one person that
shows you that it's
okay to let your guard
down, be yourself, and
love with no regrets.

What if the question is not why am
I so infrequently the person I really want
to be, but why do I so infrequently want
to be the person I really am?
~Oriah Mountain Dreamer, *The Dance*

The wind of divine grace
is always blowing.
You just need
to spread your sail.
~Swami Vivekananda

When I look back
on my life, I see pain,
mistakes and heart
ache. When I look
in the mirror,
I see strength, learned
lessons, and
pride in myself.

Life is too
short to spend it
with people who
don't make you
happy.

When you have to start
compromising yourself or
your morals for the
people around you, it's
probably time to change
the people around you.

I am brave because
I have been afraid.
I am wise because
I've made mistakes.
I can love others
because I've learned to
respect myself.

Love needs two things it has to be rooted in freedom and it has to know the art of trust. It these two things are made available your life immediately starts blossoming as if suddenly spring has come.

Osho

Mastering others is strength.

Mastering yourself is true power.

Lao Tzu

Your heart is full of fertile seeds,

waiting to sprout.

Morihei Ueshiba

"A heart filled with love
is like a phoenix that
no cage can imprison."

Rumi

Freedom

is

being

yourself

WITHOUT PERMISSION.

You May be gone from my sight...
But you are never gone from my
heart

It is not the end of the physical body that should worry us. Rather, our concern must be to live while we're alive –
to release our inner selves
from the spiritual death
that comes with living
behind a facade designed
to conform to external
definitions of who & what
we are.

~Elizabeth Kubler-Ross

Fear is the memory of Pain.
Addiction is the memory of Pleasure.
Freedom is beyond both.

Don't allow your words to transform
you into someone you are not.
Paulo Coelho

Listen carefully to how a person
speaks about other people to you. This
is how they will speak about you to
other people,

Be still. Take gentle breaths and fall in
love with life again.

I've learned that people will forget what you said, people will forget what you did, but people will never forget how you made them feel.

Maya Angelou

*Love recognizes no barriers.
It jumps hurdles, leaps fences,
penetrates walls to arrive at its
destination*

full of hope.

If you're just going through the emotions, and not feelings the emotions. You're missing the point. You're missing life.

Go confidently in the direction of your dreams Live the life you have imagined.

Henry D. Thoreau

"I see possibilities in everything. For everything that's taken away, something of greater value has been given."

Michael J. Fox Actor living with Parkinsons

"Success is liking yourself, liking what you do, and liking how you do it".

Maya Angelou

We do not grow absolutely, chronologically. We grow sometimes in one dimension,& not in another; unevenly. We grow partially. We are relative. We are mature in one realm, childish in another. . .We are made up of layers, cells, constellations.

~Anais Nin

The closer you get to excellence in your life, the more friends you'll lose. People love you when you're average because it makes them feel comfortable. But when you pursue greatness it makes people uncomfortable. Be prepared to lose some people on your journey.

Politeness has become so rare that some people mistake it for flirtation.

I hope you lived a life you're proud of. If you find that you're not, I hope you have the strength to start all over again.

F. Scott Fitzgerald

Never waste your time trying to explain who you are to people who are committed to misunderstanding you.

rawforbeauty.com

The people that are there for you on your darkest nights are the ones worth spending your brightest days with.

Lessons Learned in Life

"Just as a snake sheds its skin we must shed our past over and over again." Buddha

Today I close the door to the past, open the door to the future, take a deep breath, step on through and start a new chapter in my life.

We can never obtain peace in the outer world until we make peace with ourselves.

Dalai Lama

Not everyone will understand your journey. That's fine it's not their journey to make sense of. It's Yours'.

Never allow loneliness to drive you back into the arms of someone you know you don't belong with.

Miracles seem to rest,
not so much upon faces
or voices or healing power
coming suddenly near to us from far off,
but upon our perceptions being made finer
so that for a moment our eyes can see
and our ears can hear
that which is about us always.

~Willa Cather~

As you waste your breath complaining about life someone out there is breathing their last. Appreciate what you have. Be thankful and stop complaining. Live more, complain less. Have more smiles, less stress.

I don't engage in acts of kindness to be rewarded later. I engage in acts of kindness because it makes me feel good to give.

Millions of flowers open without forcing the buds. It reminds us not to force anything for things happen in the right time.

True love doesn't just fill your heart, it over flows into your whole body and soul.

Reputation is for time;
Character is for eternity.
J. B. Gough

The cells in your body react to everything that your mind says/ Negativity brings down your immune system.

Cutting people out of my life does not mean I hate them. It simply means I respect me.

I never make the same mistake twice. I make it like 5 or 6 times, you know, just to be sure.

"Do you want to know what my secret is? You see, I don't mind what happens." **Krishnamurti**

RELAX -
Nothing is under control.

Love me without fear.
Trust me with questioning.

Need me without demanding.
Want me without restrictions.
Accept me with change.
Desire me without inhibitions.
For a love so free will never fly away.

"Being too realistic kills your dreams."
Martin Soulreader

At the end of the day, the only
questions I will ask myself are...Did I
love enough? Did I laugh enough?
Did I make a difference.

"If you knew how many hearts are healed and how many lives are transformed throughout the patterns created in every choice, you'd follow your heart in every breath and bless the world wherever you go."

~ Matt Kahn

When the Power of love is great than the love of power. The world will know peace.

Inner peace the moment you choose not to allow another person or event to control your emotions.

Unknown

The beginning and the end of every day should include a heartfelt THANK YOU.

A lot of the pain that we are dealing with are really only THOUGHTS.

I've found the key to happiness.
Stay away from idiots.
You are never too old to set another goal or to dream a new dream.

C. S. Lewis

When you feel that nobody loves you, nobody cares for you, everyone is ignoring you, and people are jealous of you. You should really ask yourself: Am I too Sexy?!

"I want to be around people that do things I don't want to be around people anymore that judge or talk about what people do. I want to be around people who dream. And support. And do things."

Amy Poehler

When someone
loves you,
they don't have
to say it.

You can tell
by the way they
treat you.

Only if we are still enough inside, can we become aware that there is a hidden harmony here, a sacredness.
Eckhart Tolle

"Nobody really knows how much anyone else is hurting we could be standing next to someone who is completely broken and we'd never know. So, be kind always, with yourself and with others.

You are where you need to be.
Just breathe.
David Avocado Wolfe

You know great things are coming when everything seems to be going wrong. Old energy is clearing out for new energy to enter. Be Patient!

Idil Ahmed

We are all visitors to this time, this place. We are just passing through. Our purpose here is to observe to learn, to grow, to love... and then we return home.

Australian Aboriginal Proverb

Stand up for what is right, even if you are standing alone.

Native American

Why Should we only "Rest in Peace?"

Why don't we love in peace too?

More Crazy sh it

I love my curves, my tattoos, my imperfections and my jiggling thighs. No one said you had to.

Life is a Bitch Quotes

Sometimes you just have to remove people without warning.

We're getting too old to be explaining what they already know they're doing wrong.

Sun Gazing

You can't change how people treat you or what they say about you. All you can do is change how you react to it.

Mahatma Gandhi

As you awaken, you will come to understand that the journey to love isn't about finding "the one", the journey is about becoming "the one".

Creig Crippen

Not every day is a good day, live anyway. Not all you love will love back, love anyway. Not everyone will tell the truth, be honest anyway. Not all deals are fair, play fair anyway..

Higher Perspective

No one is going to stand up at your funeral and sat "She had a really expensive couch and great shoes." Don't make life about stuff.

The Idealist

We do not heal the past by dwelling there; we heal the past by living fully in the present.

Marianne Willamson

Be Strong when you are weak. Be Brave when you are scared. Be Humble when you are victorious.

Native American Pride

The World

The world is increasingly designed to depress us. Happiness isn't very good for the economy. If we were happy with what we had, why would we need more? How do you sell an anti-aging moisturiser? You make someone worry about ageing. How do you get people to vote for a political party? You make them worry about the immigration. How do you get them to buy insurance? By making them worry about everything. How do you get them to have plastic surgery? By highlighting their physical flaws. How do you get them to watch a TV show? By making them worry about missing out. How do you get them to buy a new smart phone? By making *them feel like they are being left behind.*

To be calm becomes a kind of revolutionary act. To be happy with your own non-upgraded existence. To be comfortable with our messy, human selves, would not be good for business.

Page 189

Book: 'Reasons to Stay Alive'

By Matt Haig

A person's energy can tell you more about them than their own words.

Lamanda Brown

If you have been brutally broken, but still have the courage to be gentle to others, then you deserve a love deeper than the ocean itself.

Nikita Gill

When your faith becomes stronger than your fears, then your dreams can become a reality.

BillyCox.com

If love doesn't make you a little bit crazy – then you're just not doing it right.

P. T. Berkey

Try not to confuse "attachment" with "love". Attachment is about fear and dependency, and has more to do with love of self than love of another. Love without attachment is the purest love because it isn't about what others can give you because you're empty. It is about what you can give others because you're already full.

Quantum World

"Happiness comes when you believe in what you are doing. Know what you are doing, and love what you are doing."

Brian Tracy

Keanu Reeves Just Shook the World with Another Powerful Message

By Lara Starr July 18 2016

The Earth Child

Every few months the reclusive actor opens up and offers some insights about life. This one is the latest. Enjoy...

.

"I cannot be part of a world where men dress their wives as prostitutes by showing everything that should be cherished. Where there is no concept of honor and dignity, and one can only reply on those when they say "I promise'.

Where women do not want children, and men don't want a family.

Where the suckers believe themselves to be successful behind the wheel of their fathers' car, and a father who has a little bit of power is trying to prove to you that you're a nobody.

Where people falsely declare that they believe in God with a shot of alcohol in their hand, and the lack of any understanding of their religion.

Where the concept of jealousy is considered shameful, and modesty is a disadvantage.

Where people forgot about love, but are simply looking for the best partner.

Where people repair every rustle of their car, not sparing any money or time, and themselves, they look so poor that only an expensive car can hide it.

Where the boys waste their parents money in nightclubs, aping under the primitive sounds, and girls fall in love with them for this.

Where men and women are no longer identifiable and where all this together is called freedom of choice, but for those who choose a different path-get branded as retarded despots.

I choose my path, but it's a pity that I did not find similar understanding in the people among whom I wished to find it most of all..."

Keanu Reeves

Don't worry if people don't like you. Most people are struggling to like themselves.

Mindset of Greatness

Some people will only love you of you fit into their box...

Don't be afraid to disappoint.

Facebook/Dil Transcend

If it is complicated, it's from ego. Spirit is simple.

www.soul-process.com

"Returning violence for violence multiplies violence, adding a deeper darkness to a night already devoid of stars. Darkness cannot drive out darkness: only love can do that. Hate cannot drive out hate: only love can do that.

Martin Luther King

People who are spiritually minded tend to suffer from anxiety and depression more. But this is because their eyes are open to a world that is in need of repair. They literally have an increased ability to feel the emotions of people around them.

Quantum World

People think you're crazy if you talk about things they don't understand.

As you evolve you will make a lot of people uncomfortable.

Evolve Anyway.

Soulogy One Studios

No amount of guilt can change the past and no amount of worrying can change the future.

Insight Timer

They may not be avoiding you. They may just be:

1. Distracted by a sudden life change.
2. Working hard to make ends meet or to make sense of their situation.
3. Too worn out to socialize
4. Dealing with personal pain or illness.
5. Tired of having to pretend to be okay around you when they're really doing all they can to survive.

Don't Make Snap Judgements.

You Just Never Know.

FB David Avocado Wolfe

Detox your life in 4 east steps

Eliminate anyone who:

1.   Lies to you.
2.   Disrespects you.
3.   Uses you.
4.   Puts you down.

Spirit Science
Archann.net

Stop creating a life that you need a vacation from. Instead, move to where you want to live, do what you want to do, start what you want to start, and create the life you want today. This isn't rehearsal people. This is your life.

Dale Partridge

You seriously have no idea what people are dealing with in their private lie, so just be nice. It's that simple!

Advanced Life Skills.com

When you find people who not only tolerate your quirks but celebrate them with glad cries of "me too!" be sure to cherish them. Because those weirdos are your tribe.

Simple Organic Life

You don't realize how badly you've been treated until someone comes along and treats you the way you should be treated.

Lulu's Secret Desires

Transformation is the journey you are on. You are exploring the wisdom of your soul. You are shedding old ways and beliefs that no longer fit who you are becoming.

Be brave, dear one you are becoming your authentic self!

Diana Moore

You will never be good enough for everybody, but you will always be the nest for someone who really appreciates you.

1,000,000 Quotes

The best apology is change behaviour.

1,000,000 Quotes

"The spiritual journey is individual, highly personal. It can't be organized or regulated. It isn't true that everyone should follow one path. Listen to your own truth."

Ram Dass

It all begins and ends in your mind what you give power to, has power over you.

Leon Brown

It takes one word to destroy someone's life, and one minute to make someone's day.

BE KIND

Don't let someone who did you wrong make you think there's something wrong with you. Don't devalue yourself because they didn't value you. Know your worth even if they don't.

@TrentShelton

The eye sees only what the mind is prepared to comprehend.

FB Lauren Kurth

Man is the most insane species. He worships an invisible God and slaughters a visible Nature... without realizing that this Nature he slaughters is this invisible God he worships.

Hubert Reeves

I believe that the only true religion consists of having a good heart.

Dalai Lama

You are rich, when you are content and happy with what you have.

www.soul-process.com

"I am old but I am forever young at heart. We are always the same age inside. Know that you are the perfect age. Each year is special and precious, you can only live it once. Do not regret growing older, it's a privilege denied to many!"

Richard Gere

No one is born hating another person because of the colour of his skin, or his background or his religion. People learn to hate, and if they can learn to hate, they can be taught to love, for love comes more naturally to the human heart than it opposite.

Nelson Mandela

Cheers to all the people who just want to be themselves and don't care about fitting in.

Spirit Science

Truth is available only to those who have the courage to question whatever they have been taught.

FB Ginny Jones

It might take a year, it might take a day, but what's meant to be will always find its way.

Power of Positivity

Timing is everything. The things you are praying for will show up when you are most ready for them.

Power of Positivity

When you understand that what most people really, really want is simply to feel good about themselves, and when you realize that with just a few well-chosen words you can help virtually anyone on the planet instantly achieve this, you being to realize just how simple life is, how powerful you are, and that

love is the key.

Mike Dooley

All relationships have one law. Never make the one you love feel alone, especially when you're there.

Power of Positivity

To be beautiful means to be yourself. You don't need to be accepted by others you need to accept yourself.

Thich Nhat Hanh

The sad thing is, nobody ever really knows how much anyone else is hurting. We could be standing next to somebody who is completely broken and we wouldn't even know it.

Sun-gazing.com

In a world where you can be anything: Be Kind

Power of Positivity

Growth is painful. Change is painful. But nothing is as painful as staying stuck somewhere you don't belong.

Kushandwizdom.tumblr.com

Maturity

is learning to walk away

from people and situations that threaten your peace of mind,

self-respect, values, morals,

or self-worth.

WomenWorking.com

The more you thank life, the more life gives you to be thankful for.

Power of Positivity

Your perception

of me is a reflection of you;

my reaction to you

is an awareness of me.

FB Ginny Jones

Stop over thinking.

You can't control everything.

Just let it be.

FB Peace Summer Life

Be open to everything and

attached to nothing.

FB Dil Transcend

The greatest gift you give someone is your time. Because when you give your time you are giving a portion of your life that you will never get back.

1,000,000 Quotes

"Children must be taught

How to Think

not what to think."

Margaret Mead

Your mind will always believe
everything you tell it. Feed it hope.
Feed it truth. Feed it with Love.

FB David Newman aka Durga Das

Fate whispers to the warrior

"You cannot withstand the storm,"

and the warrior whispers back

"I am the storm."

FB Dil Transcend

Don't waste your time with
explanations. People only what they
want to hear.

Paulo Coelho

When a toxic person can no longer control you, they will try to control how others see you. The misinformation will feel unfair, but <u>stay</u> <u>above</u> <u>it</u>, trusting that other people will eventually see the <u>truth</u>, just like you did.

Crowfeather

Don't underestimate me. I know more than I say, think more than I speak, & notice more than you realize

Spirit Science

Archann.Net

Empaths be like...

I don't just listen to your words

I listen to your use of words, your tone, your body movements, your eyes, your subtle facial expressions.

I interpret your silences – I can hear everything you don't say in words.

Higher Perspective

Whatever you think about activates a vibration within you.

www.ginnyjoneshealing.com

If someone treats you badly, just remember that there is something wrong with them, not you. Normal people don't go around destroying other human beings.

The Law of Attraction

"When I run after what I think I want, my days are a furnace of stress and anxiety; if I sit in my own place of patience, what I need flows to me, and without pain. From this I understand that what I want also wants me, is looking for me and attracting me. There is a great secret here for anyone who can grasp it."

Rumi

A Buddhist Prayer of Forgiveness

If I have harmed anyone in any way
either knowingly or unknowingly
through my own confusions I ask
their forgiveness.
If anyone has harmed me in any way
either knowingly or unknowingly
through their own confusions
I forgive them.
And if there is a situation I am not yet
ready to forgive I forgive myself for
that.
For all the ways that I harm myself,
negate, doubt, belittle myself, judge or
be unkind to myself through my own
confusions. I forgive myself.

FB Jorge Alejandro Allende –
Lightworkers of the World

1.   *Everything happens for a reason.*

2.   *To live and die without regret.*

3.   *Unconditional Love*

1.   *Learn from Yesterday*

2.   *Live for Today*

3.   *Hope for Tomorrow*

Words I do my best to live by.

From Tibetan Drutsa Script

Renee Henderson

Bibliography

Facebook/Words to Ponder

Facebook/The Mind Unleashed

Facebook/Carolyn Smith

Facebook/LIORA

Facebook/Jill Blakeway

Facebook/Angel Intuitive

Facebook/www.enlighteningquotes.com

Facebook/Out of the Ashes

Facebook/Positively Positive

Facebook/livelifehappy.com

Facebook/Pink

Facebook/Hay House Writers Workshops

Facebook/Maya Angelou

Facebook/OnePlanetOnePlace.com

Facebook/Mark Alana Effingers

Facebook/Clairporium.com

Facebook/Patientlikeme

Facebook/The Rockettes

Facebook/Soulmates – Twinflames

Facebook/Tony A. Gaskins Jr.

Facebook/rawforbeauty.com

Facebook/Mystera Magazine

Facebook/LessonsLearnedInLife

Facebook/James van Praagh

Facebook/A Place to Reflect

Facebook/Chris Burke

Facebook/www.livelifehappy.com

Facebook/Nonpoint

Facebook/Ebook Korner Kafe

Facebook/Korner Kafe

Facebook/444fairies

Facebook/Arslane Youssef

Facebook/Baisden Live

Facebook/ Comedy 103.1

Facebook/PreventDisease.com

Facebook/Martin Soulreader

Facebook/Simple Reminders

Facebook/Wisdom Seekers

Facebook/Transcend

Facebook/Alice 105.9

Facebook/Pachamama Alliance

Facebook/Angel Falls

Facebook/MomsRising.org

Facebook/Growing Bolder

Facebook/Enchanting Minds

Facebook/Tyrese Gibson

Facebook/Blue Cure

Facebook/Pamela Kist

Facebook/Shift of the Ages

Facebook/Psychic Medium Michelle Russell

Facebook/Christi Paul

Facebook/Fife and Dave

Facebook/Quotes and Thoughts

Facebook/Make the World a Better Place

Facebook/Deepak Chopra

Facebook/Shashicka Tyre-Hill

Facebook/Crystal Blackburn Medium,

Facebook/Angel Advisor

Facebook/Jack Canfield

Facebook/Marcos Via

Facebook/Sue Fitzmaurice Author

Facebook/The ManKind Project

Facebook/WomenWorking.com

Facebook/Power 103.5 FM – O'City

Facebook/The Dalai Lama in Australia

Facebook/TheAfterlifeofBillyFingers

Facebook/Ginny Jones Spiritual Artist

Facebook/Springwood Wellness Centre

Facebook/Super Soul Sunday

Facebook/Deb Rowley

Facebook/Herty Borngreat Music

Facebook/Loving Angel Messages

Facebook/Md Wraihan Khan

Facebook/Just Being

Facebook/humanityhealing.net

Facebook/Hay House (1)

Facebook/Pat Armitstead

Facebook/www.livelifehappy.com

Facebook/Karen Salmonsohn

Facebook/94.9 The Bull

Facebook/Psychic Alex

Facebook/ Kendyl Eadie

Facebook/ Anna Taylor

Facebook/ Positive Outlooks

Facebook/ MISS 103

Facebook/Love, Sex, Intelligence

Facebook/Ben Gunnell

Facebook/Dancing-With Spirit

Facebook/Oriah Mountain Dreamer

Facebook/www.theartthechild.co.za – Keanu Reeves

Facebook/Suyog Mhadgut - -Namaste

Facebook/Andrew Harvey- Author

Facebook/Native American World

Facebook/More Crazy sh it

Facebook/Life is a Bitch Quotes with Like Beauty

Facebook/Sun Gazing

Facebook/Visvanath Das

Facebook/Getrude Matshe

Facebook/The Idealist

Facebook/Spiritual Events Directory

Facebook/Native American Pride

Facebook/Lamanda Brown

Facebook/Aura & Soul Psychology

Facebook/Quantum World: Awaken Your Mind with Kayla Miller and Jennifer Freeman

Facebook/Evolver Social Movement – Mindset of Greatness

Facebook/Spirit Science – ARCHANN.NET

Facebook/Crowfeather Psychic Medium

Facebook/Paulo Coelho

Facebook/David Newman aka Durga Das

Facebook/ John Howe
LIGHTWORKERS of THE WORLD

Facebook/Tina Malia

www.ginnyjoneshealing.com

Facebook/1,000,000 Quotes

Facebook/Jorge Alejandro Allende –
LIGHTWORKERS of THE WORLD

Facebook/Power of Positivity

Facebook/Native American Clothing & Accessories

Facebook/ Spiritual Bless – Richard Gere

Facebook/ Anna Morten

Facebook/Lauren Kurth

Facebook/Open Heart Place

Facebook/Famous Quotes

www.Awesomequotes4u.com

Facebook/Diana Moore

Facebook/My Baby Daddy Aint Shit

Facebook/Simple Organic Life

Facebook/ Alan R J Moffitt Dspooky1nz

Facebook/Harper Pollock with Kurt Johnson

Artist: Archan Nair

Facebook. Insight Timer

Facebook/Soulogy One Studios

Facebook/Crystal Heart & Soul

Facebook/Occupy Democrats – Martin Luther King

www.soul-process.com

Facebook/Paul E McAtarsney Author

Facebook/Dil Transcend

Facebook/Renee Henderson

www.guardianhouse.tumblr.com

Pinterest/Renee Henderson

www.ingramcontent.com/pod-product-compliance
Lightning Source LLC
Chambersburg PA
CBHW051945090426
42741CB00008B/1278